George Alexander
1808 - 1813

The Beautiful Spotted Boy

George Alexander Gratton
1808-1813

Jacqueline Roberts
Copyright ©2020

First Edition Published by SV2G - Jacqueline Roberts

Copyright ©2020 SV2G - Jacqueline Roberts

WOW Book Publishing™

All rights reserved. Neither this book, nor any parts within it, may be sold or reproduced in any form without permission.

No part of this book may be reproduced in any form or by any electronic or mechanical means including information storage and retrieval systems, without permission in writing from the author. The only exception is by a reviewer, who may quote short excerpts in a review.

The purpose of this book is to educate. The opinions and views expressed in this book are that of the author based on the research conducted by the SV2G Project.

Neither the author, nor SV2G; shall neither be liable; nor responsible for any loss nor damage allegedly arising from any information in this book.

Dedication

This book is dedicated to Vincentian Nationals home and abroad to understand our historical presence in Britain.

Table of Contents

Acknowledgments 7
Testimonials 9
Foreword 13
Preface 15

Land of the Blessed 19
   St. Vincent and the Grenadines 19
   Sir William Young, 1st Baronet (1724/5 – 1788)...............23
   Sir William Young 2nd Baronet...26
   Plantation Life 29
   Chief Joseph Chatoyer 39

The Enslaved Journey to Britain 43
   Crossing the Atlantic 43
   Britain and its Spotted Boy...53

Table of Contents

Human Commodity 57

George Alexander Gratton - "The Spotted Boy" 57
Richardson's Spotted Boy Gimmick 61
Life in Richardson's care for George 64
Piebaldism 67

A 'Live Curiosity Piece' to be seen 69

John Richardson – The Showman 69
Marlow, Buckinghamshire 71
Bartholomew Fair 73
Portrait Commissions of George Alexander Gratton 79

Death and Burial 84

The Royal College of Surgeons 84
Epitaphs and Inscriptions 89
Conservation, Memorial and Plaque 92
John Richardson's Death and Will 95
Removal of the grave 96

Timeline 99
Bibliography 101

Acknowledgments

Firstly, we acknowledge the souls of our ancestors that are no longer here.

In this book, we acknowledge the communities of High Wycombe and Marlow for their participation in the SV2G's 18th century Vincentian Presence in Marlow, Buckinghamshire project.

Thanks and appreciation to the Marlow Museum, Marlow Society, Marlow All Saints Church, the Oxford Diocese, GEM Conservation; Story Finders, Dr Roger Bowdler, and Dr Adrian Fraser for their support and for providing the detailed information for both the project and this book for which we thank each and everyone involved.

Our deep gratitude to the late Dr Edgar Adams for the donation of his research as well as for contributing his published books to SV2G's project; the contribution has been invaluable.

Acknowledgments

We would also like to acknowledge our gratitude to the National Lottery Heritage Fund (NLHF) for their continued support and grant towards this project.

We are indebted to the Officiators Bishop Melvin Brooks and Bishop Memory Tapfumaneyi for the Service and Unveiling of George's Headstone and Plaque.

Sincere thanks to Vishal Morjaria at WOW Publishing™ for his leadership and also Author and Book Angel Pauline Barath for her continued dedicated support to ensure this book was completed.

Testimonials

"Bishop Melvin Brooks and I were privileged to be invited by Jacqueline and the SV2G Trustees to officiate at the service and unveiling of George's headstone and Plaque, prior to this l did not know much about George's life and most importantly his journey to England at a tender age of fifteen months.

This book brings in-depth knowledge and history about Georges' subsequent life and conditions he was subjected to and made to live and endure in the four years of his life until his untimely death.

The book also causes a mixture of emotions when one reads about the historical narratives of those enslaved in St. Vincent and the Grenadines. To imagine a fifteen-month-old baby had his relationship severed with his parents and moved thousands of miles to a totally different environment and people to what he had known in his formative years reveals the inhuman and cruelty of the Trans-Atlantic Slave Trade.

The book reveals how those enslaved were treated as objects and in the case of George an amusement and

Testimonials

money-making entity. The horror that George was made to work long hours and displayed to all sectors of the community is heartbreaking.

The change of environment, the trauma that he suffered due to the separation from his family, the journey to England and the long hours of work for this four-year-old child meant that his life was tragically shortened leading to his death.

This information is captured, evidenced and cross-referenced with other scholarly and historical materials showing the richness, academic robustness, diligence and passion Jacqueline and SV2G Researchers did on this project. I commend them for this outstanding work and recommend that this book be added to the history reading lists in schools and places of higher learning."

Bishop Memory Tapfumaneyi

"This book offers a unique insight into the story of the child George Alexander Gratton taken from his homeland, the island of St Vincent. It allows his silent voice and perspective to be at the forefront of the narrative to inform and engage readers."

Abigail Bernard,
Researcher/Oral Historian

"This unique look into George's life is not only unbiased, but caring and open-minded. Jacqueline and the researchers of the SV2G project have really focused on the people and their actions that impacted George's life, either directly or indirectly.

Their compassion for both sides of the story, the heroes and the villains; as well as the questions they have posed to find the truth about this young boy's life, are both inspiring, and informative.

Told like no other records, this book not only brings George's life into the spotlight once again, but for the first time he is identified as the exploited child that he was. Not the spotted boy, not the slave...

But George Alexander Gratton, the child that was stripped of ordinary privileges that most people take for granted; I commend Jacqueline for her hard work on this book and look forward to seeing what further research the SV2G uncovers in the future."

Pauline Barath
Author and Book Angel,

Foreword

St. Vincent and the Grenadines 2nd Generation (SV2G) initiated a heritage project, due to the timely concerns about the advanced deterioration and partial loss of George Alexander Gratton's headstone. The importance of documenting one's history is of great importance before it is lost.

This book has successfully raised awareness for one of the earliest arrivals of Vincentian presence in Britain. Jacqueline Roberts has managed to capture the essence of this tragic story from the research uncovered from the SV2G project.

This book has not only documented George's existence that has been long overlooked, but it also serves as a significant contribution to Black history in Britain.

Vishal Morjaria
Award Winning Author, Publisher,
And International Speaker

Preface

The tragic story of George Alexander Gratton (1808-1813) is brought to you by the community research led by St. Vincent and the Grenadines 2nd Generation (SV2G).

"Revisiting 18th-century Vincentian presence in Marlow", was a Heritage lottery-funded project based on the preservation of the grave of George also known as the 'Extraordinary Beautiful Spotted Boy' in Marlow, Buckinghamshire. The project uncovered the Marlow Town and the wider Buckinghamshire connections to the Vincentian community in the Wycombe District.

High Wycombe has the largest concentration of Vincentian's living in the UK of which is where SV2G is based. Vincentians in the Wycombe District are made up largely of Indo-Vincentians'. Many Indo-Vincentians that were descendants of Indian indentured labourers migrated from St. Vincent where they first settled in the early 19th century.

The black community in Buckinghamshire can be found in the medieval period. The first known black person is registered in the baptism records in

Preface

Hedgerley in 1607. During the late 18th-century and early 19th-century, it was also evident of black people working in the fairs that would travel through High Wycombe and Marlow, as well as being domestic servants.

Many Buckinghamshire families that were wealthy land-owners were also slave plantation owners or shareholders in the Caribbean. It is most likely that these families would have transported their slaves to their homes in Buckinghamshire as their personal servants. This is demonstrated in the painting of Sir William Young and his family at Delaford House in the following chapters of this book.

As part of the project, SV2G commissioned GEM conservation to restore the derelict condition of the grave. The untold tragic story of George Alexander Gratton, which reveals his short life and the country of his birth, remained dormant until SV2G raised awareness over several years and finally raised the funds to preserve his grave to secure Vincentian history in Britain.

Significantly, his grave is one of, if not the earliest, pieces of evidence of Vincentian presence in Britain. Many people have been captivated by this unique story of an enslaved African child who was born into slavery in St. Vincent and the Grenadines, and taken from his homeland and transported to England to be displayed as "a live curiosity piece".

There are a number of conflicting stories about George that can be found online where these stories have been retold and rewritten in blogs, articles and on various websites.

Although the exact circumstances under which or how George arrived in Britain are unknown. This book will give the reader an insight into Black presence in Georgian Britain and an understanding of how an enslaved African child from St. Vincent became the property of a workhouse orphan from Marlow, Buckinghamshire.

The importance of the project and this book is as an instrumental source for Black history to preserve and share. SV2G is an African and Caribbean organisation that raises awareness through the arts, heritage and culture.

SV2G has also created a website to serve as a legacy for George Alexander Gratton. Funds raised by this book and other donations received will support the creative and preventative work with

Preface

children and young people allowing them to, unlike George, enjoy a positive start in life.

"The memorial itself embodies the poignance of George Gratton's story and that the themes of slavery, enforced migration and ultimately love and redemption are entirely spiritually relevant today."

Advisory Committee, Diocese of Oxford

Land of the Blessed

St. Vincent and the Grenadines

St. Vincent and the Grenadines comprises of thirty-two islands, islets, and cays that lie within the Lesser Antilles in the Eastern Caribbean Sea.

Archaeological evidence suggests that the first groups of people to settle in St. Vincent were the Amerindians known as the Ciboneys about 5000B.C.

The evidence also suggests that they then followed the Taino's who were part of the Arawakan speaking group of people in the first century A.D. It is believed that the Kalinago's arrived in St. Vincent between 100 AD and 1400.

Over centuries St. Vincent & the Grenadines were known to have various names, in British literature when Christopher Columbus visited in 1498 on his 4th voyage, the name was given after the patron Saint Vincent of Saragossa whose feast day falls on the 22nd January. According to Adams (2002), St. Vincent and the Grenadines was known as 'Youlou and Begos' to the indigenous Kalinago people.

It is also uncertain in historical literature when the name Hairouna, meaning 'Land of the Blessed' was introduced. The Garinagu people today still refer to St. Vincent as Youloumain, Yurumein and or spelt as Youromayn meaning 'Motherland' in the Garifuna culture.

The French were the first Europeans to occupy St. Vincent exporting sugar, tobacco amongst various other commodities. African traders were also present long before the first arrival of Christopher Columbus in the West Indies.

The 'British Calendar of State Papers' (1661-1668) St. Vincent has people of African descent as early as 1635 when two Spanish slave vessels were lost and landed in the Grenadines.

Also, in 1675, a Dutch slave vessel named 'Palmira' was shipwrecked on Bequia. It is believed the Kalinago people assisted them on-shore and from the integration of both groups within the community, their descendants were known as Garifuna, also known as Garinagu people.

Today, we now question whether the Garifuna's were from the interrelations of Africans and Kalinago's but were in fact a pure race of the people already residing in St. Vincent.

The research to substantiate this is currently being led by the Central American Black Organisation.

It is believed that George was from the Garifuna community who were removed by the British which caused many of them to lose their Garifuna culture over the years in St. Vincent. However, those that were exiled maintained their indigenous language and cultural traditions.

Also, four hundred and sixteen Garifuna fighters and their families were part of the two-thousand-five-hundred-and-twelve people taken from the Caribbean as prisoners of war to Portchester castle in England in 1796.

Following a number of wars and signed treaties, St. Vincent was eventually relinquished to the British under the 1783 treaty of Versailles. The indigenous people of St. Vincent continued to defend their lands with two Caribs wars over a period of several years with the French against the British.

After the second Carib war in 1795, following the death of Paramount Chief Joseph Chatoyer, St. Vincent and the Grenadines was fully colonised by the British in 1797.

The surviving fighters, mainly Garifuna's, known by the British colonists as Black Caribs were exiled to Roatan, an island off the coast of Honduras now known as Belize. This may have affected the course of George's life leading him down a path of slavery.

Although the British Slave Trade was abolished on 28th August 1833 by Royal assent, enslaved people over the age of six years old still had to work unpaid under an apprenticeship scheme.

Full emancipation only became law on 1 August 1838. For many indigenous people in St. Vincent and the Grenadines, their story has been lost because several decades passed with limited historical accounts that have been made public.

British historians acknowledged two published works to be influential in shaping the thinking and debates on the Carib wars. These works were published in 1795 by Sir William Young 2nd Baronet who edited his father's papers Sir William Young the 1st Baronet, on the British Carib conflict and Charles Shephard in 1831 of his version of 'a historical account of St. Vincent'.

However, many historians today argue of the biases in which these works have been written from a colonial perspective. According to Fraser (2019), it is a continuing story of our history to be fully told with the available works from the French Missionaries and envoys in St. Vincent during the Carib wars that have exposed the conflicting perspectives of colonial writers. There are many scholars globally, to whom we are thankful for their research and continuous work to recover and correct our history.

Sir William Young, 1st Baronet (1724/5 – 1788)

Sir William Young Baronet of Delaford, Buckinghamshire Sir William Young, 1st Baronet (1724/5 – 1788), was the Governor of Dominica and the Chief Commissioner for the ceded lands in Dominica, Grenada, St. Vincent and in Tobago after the treaty of Paris in 1763. As the Chief Commissioner for distributed lands, Young, 1st acquired land in Dominica, Tobago and in St. Vincent for himself.

The Pembrook and the Calliaqua (included Villa) estates became part of his fortune along with two unnamed estates in Bequia. According to Taylor (2012), Young 1st made 110 voyages within nine years during his time commissioning lands.

It is alleged that the island that is known today as Young's Island was owned by Sir William Young exchanged two horses or as other sources state a white horse to the Paramount Chief Joseph Chatoyer for ownership of the Island.

Carib lands were traditionally under communal ownership of the people and therefore it has been regarded by many that such an exchange should never have taken place between Young and Chatoyer for their own personal gain (Adams 2002, Fraser 2019). It is noted that Brunais also featured Young Island with Sir William Young in his paintings and Chatoyer and his wives.

Sir William Young died on 8 April 1788 in St Vincent, leaving his estate to his eldest son who was also named William, and became Sir William Young, 2nd Baronet.

The picture on the next page depicts Sir William Young 1st Bt and his family with John Brook, an enslaved young man from one of Young's plantation who was brought to England.

Find an in-depth look into Sir William's impact on St. Vincent in the 1700s by visiting
**www.sv2g.org.uk /
www.georgealexandergratton.com**

The Beautiful Spotted Boy

Painted by Johann Zoffany, 1767-17694

Courtesy of the Walker Art Gallery

Sir William Young 2nd Baronet

In 1788, Sir William Young the 2nd Baronet of Delaford, Buckinghamshire inherited his father's estates in the Caribbean along with his father's debts owed to the British Government.

Young became the owner of four estates, one in Antigua, two in St. Vincent, and one in Tobago that were managed by his brother in law Bryan Edwards who later published his tour visiting the West Indies. Hartwell House, Buckinghamshire was a former residence for Young.

Young, the 2nd Baronet, was an advocate of British Imperialism. He served as the secretary to the 'Association for Promoting the Discovery of the Interior Parts of Africa'. His conservative attitude towards abolition could be due to the inherited debt from his father as abolition would only deteriorate his financial circumstances.

With his financial uncertainty he became a prominent pro-slavery campaigner in the House of Commons. He spoke aggressively with an abundance of rudeness and made outrageous claims against William Wilberforce's proposal for the abolition of slavery.

It can also be argued that his conservative attitude to the abolition of the slave trade could be his reasons to sustain his new wealth from slavery.

On the 19th April 1791 Young gave a speech in parliament opposing Wilberforce slave trade abolition campaign condemning and citing it as a sacrifice that would be "a considerable portion of British commerce and an ultimate surrender of the British colonies" On the 26th February 1793, Young reported on his observations from his tour of the West Indies when he led against Wilberforce's motion on the slave trade.

His further obstructions against the abolition campaign were also noted on 15 March 1796 at the reporting phase of the abolition bill where he objected to every point considered.

Young became an agent also known as a land Commissioner in 1795 – 1802 in St. Vincent and in 1807 became the Governor of Dominica and Tobago. Young also published 'The West Indian Commonplace book in 1807, a detailed assessment of the West Indies for British colonial interests.

Young also served as an MP in Buckingham in 1806, then was appointed Governor of Tobago in 1807 until his death and had many other connections in Buckinghamshire for this reason, SV2G believes many enslaved Africans from St. Vincent and the Grenadines would have been taken to England to work in the Young family's home and possibly sold to other families in Buckinghamshire.

SV2G has also discovered that there are many other links to slavery from plantations in St. Vincent and the wider Caribbean linked to former residents in Buckinghamshire.

Had Young's politics been slightly different, George's carer, John Richardson, would have been less likely to so freely exploit him.

For a more in-depth look into the consequences and results of the Young family's politics and youthful decisions as well as their connections in St. Vincent visit the website www.sv2g.org.uk

Plantation Life

Plantation life in St. Vincent and the experiences of the people involved were rarely documented. Although many works available were produced by the Colonisers. In 1493, Columbus carried sugar cane on his second transatlantic voyage as sugar became very profitable for British settlers in the Caribbean.

As the plantation model became popular, the demand for slave labour increased not only for sugar but also for tobacco. Working conditions on the plantations were harsh; an organised gang system was introduced on sugar plantations. Sugar factories were built to convert the harvested sugar cane to make rum.

It was discovered that George was born on or near the Orange Hill estate in St. Vincent which is the ancestral land of the indigenous Garifuna people of St Vincent. SV2G was unable at the time of their project to confirm whether it was in fact the Colonaire Vale estate George's parents worked on.

Although tobacco plantations were smaller, the enslaved worked side by side in the salt ponds, the conditions were harsh. Many workers standing in the salt-water suffered from boils. Other enslaved people worked as domestic slaves for their owners or managers on the plantations.

Punishments and violations of the enslaved were a daily occurrence, and were the most common recollections of the enslaved people. Whilst physical abuse such as the 'lash' was frequent to force work, it was also used as a way of life.

It was also common for women and girls to be sexually abused by their owners or managers and overseers on the plantations. Other personal violations also suffered, were being removed from estates to be sold and transported without notice, leaving family members behind.

Many were transported on the Atlantic ships to ports in England with produce and other goods from the Caribbean. They were at times rented out to other men and women for other work. George was one of these unfortunates when he was sold to Showman John Richardson in England and was forced to leave St Vincent.

Little is known or documented about the experiences of the enslaved people living in St. Vincent and the Grenadines. However, Adams (2002) noted Ashton Warne's account of slavery that was taken from 'Flambeau' (1967) of the encounters endured by the enslaved in St. Vincent and the Grenadines;

"I was born on the island of St. Vincent and baptised by the name of Ashton Warner, in the parish church, by the Rev. Mr Gildon. My father and mother, at the time of my birth, were slaves on Cane Grove estate, in Bucumar Valley, then the property of Mr Ottely...

The whole gang of field slaves is divided into spells, and every man and woman able to work has not only to endure during crop-time the severe daily labour, but to work half the night also, or three whole nights in the week.

The work is very severe, and great numbers of slaves, during this period, sink under it and become ill.

But if they complain their complaints are not readily believed, or are considered only a pretence to escape from labour. If they are so very ill that their inability to work can be no longer doubted, they are at length sent to the sick-house. The sick house is just like a pen to keep pigs in. If you wish to keep yourself clean and decent you cannot.

It is one of the greatest punishments of the slaves to be sent there. When they were pressed, and had much sugar to pot, the manager would often send to the sick-house for the people who were sick or lame with sores to help us.

If they refused to come and said that they were unable to work, they were taken down and severely flogged by the manger's order with the cart-whip. There is nothing in slavery harder to bear than this.

When you are ill and cannot work, your complaints are neither listened to nor believed. I have seen people who were so sick that they could scarcely stand, dragged out of the sick house, tied up to a tree and flogged in a shocking manner, then driven with the whip to work.

I have seen slaves in this state crawl away, and lie down among the wet trash to get a little ease though they knew it would most likely cause their deaths."

Ashton Warner, 'Flambeau' (1967)

The Beautiful Spotted Boy

Many images discovered of plantation society in the Caribbean were captured by Italian artist Agostino Brunias; who travelled with Sir William Young 1st Bt, as his personal artist. Brunias was tasked with recording the progress that Young made during his appointment as the first Commissioner for the ceded islands of Dominica, St Vincent, Grenada and Tobago in December 1764.

These islands were known as the 'Southern Caribbees' that made Brunias a key tool for Young to document his travels in the Caribbean. Brunias' works were sketches, watercolours and oil paintings on paper, canvas and wood. His work on all subjects would then be transported to Britain to be engraved as prints. It was noted that many of his works were engraved of which some of his images were reversed when transferred onto print.

His prints were popular, as his work was considered to be of a high quality regardless of his deceptive portrayal of plantation life.

A lot of Brunias' work portrays the biased view of the Young family and their pro-slavery politics. Therefore much of Brunias' art is considered to be pro-slavery propaganda for his pro-slavery clients that were mostly plantation owners during the time when the campaign to abolish the slave trade was being intensified.

Although we know some Black people were free people in St. Vincent; much debate would identify Brunias and his clients' visions of Black and Creole society were biased towards those that would commission and purchase his work.

Brunias would depict a passive colourful atmosphere as a backdrop to his paintings with enslaved people portrayed as happy and well cared for. No scenes of enslaved people in action working in the cane fields or at the sugar mills could be found in his work.

There were many accounts in the late 18th-century that described how enslaved people were forced to wear iron neck braces and metal gagging masks that were padlocked on the head as a form of punishment on the streets of Kingstown, yet these accounts are not recorded in Brunias' work.

It has been suggested that he deliberately ignored the inhuman, brutal treatment of the indigenous people in the Caribbean that he would have witnessed around him in exchange for the profit he gained and to please his clients.

The Beautiful Spotted Boy

"A Negro Festival drawn from Nature in the Island of St Vincent."

Engraved by Philip Audinet 'after Agostino Brunias (ca 1801)
By courtesy of the National Maritime Museum, Greenwich, London, Michael Graham-Stewart Slavery Collection. Acquired with the assistance of the Heritage Lottery Fund

The image on the previous page illustrates a festival on the Caribbean island of St. Vincent published in 1801, originally owned by Sir William Young Bt. This was published by Young's brother in law planter-historian Bryan Edwards in The History, Civil and Commercial, of the British Colonies in the West Indies 3rd edition.

Many free Black people were illustrated in Brunias' paintings of life that were mainly of market scenes and village life. Festivals were considered important aspects of plantation life and Brunias would portray these people dressed in expensive clothing as free people. However his paintings depicted black people dancing with an abundance of fruits and vegetation to demonstrate wealth and happiness. This is in contrast to accounts of real experiences that consisted of horrendous treatment which the enslaved endured.

When British colonial society took root in St. Vincent and the Grenadines, Brunias was viewed as an outsider, being an Italian Roman Catholic.

During this time, it was mainly the French Roman Catholics that were discriminated against as the minority in St. Vincent with the newly established Church of England.

Brunias was considered a draughtsman which would place him at the same level as Young's white servants.

It was therefore believed that Brunias would have engaged in a social life with the 'free people of colour' that were mainly the French 'Mulattoes' who also had settled into St. Vincent before British rule and who lived a life with tradesmen and owners of smaller estates.

After St Vincent, Brunias went back to Dominica to spend the rest of his life with the family he started before visiting St Vincent. He continued to paint until his death on 2 April 1796 at the age of 66.

Brunias was buried in the cemetery grounds at the Roman Catholic Church dedicated to Notre Dame du Bon Port, Our Lady of Fair Haven, in Roseau, Dominica.

SV2G discovered that during one of Brunias' visits to Britain, he had re-worked many of his Carib life paintings at Stowe House, in Buckinghamshire.

This is also in the same county where George's grave is located and the base for SV2G was established.

According to various sources, he made wall paintings in the Ante Library. However; there is no evidence of his work found by the 1870s as they were painted over.

Brunais' collective detailed paintings have become significant records of the existence of the indigenous people in the Caribbean.

Chief Joseph Chatoyer

Joseph Chatoyer, also known as Satuye, was one of the chief leaders of the Garifuna Black Caribs in St. Vincent and the Grenadines. Chatoyer was known as a freedom fighter that led his people into battle against the British.

Oil painting of Chief Joseph Chatoyer and his wifes

Over the years the treaty agreement of Paris, in 1763 was ignored, leading to the second Carib war that took place in 1795 led by British General Sir Ralph Abercromby.

There have been several published stories of how Chatoyer allegedly died, yet little to nothing about his burial.

One account claimed that he died at the hands of Colonel Alexander Leith in a duel and that at the moment of Chatoyer's death he was grasping his silver sword that was gifted to him by King William IV who visited St. Vincent with the Navy, known then as Prince Henry.

However, Fraser (2019) argued that there was no mention of a duel in a document "Narrative of the insurrection in the Island of St. Vincent" believed to have been published in the St. Vincent Gazette in 1795. The document claimed that Chatoyer and other Carib Chiefs fell at the hands of Captain Skinner, and Lieutenant Groves.

These two Officers were praised along with Captain Campbell and Major Wytell. Fraser (2019) has also noted a letter from Governor Seton describing a similar account at Dorsetshire, St. Vincent whereby Seton singles out the bravery of

Captain Skinner, Captain Campbell and Lieutenant McIver. Again, no mention was made of Major Leith. This British account of his death is argued by many academics who believe it to be false because to this day the remains of Chatoyer are unknown.

Interestingly to note, it has been suggested in one of Brunias' paintings that it was Sir William Young that killed Chatoyer. The painting portrays Sir William Young as a hero while he kills a Carib of which others believe to be Chatoyer.

On 14 March 2002, the Paramount Chief Joseph Chatoyer (Chatawe), was declared the first National Hero of St. Vincent and the Grenadines, which also became the day for National Heroes.

On the next page; the images of Chatoyer portrayed by Brunias are the only illustrations of him during the 18th century. The painting of Chatoyer and his five wives has become a key academic reference.

Brunais depiction of Chatoyer in primitive clothes wrapped around him has also been questioned with the findings at Portchester Castle, England, where the Garifuna prisoners of war were dressed in soldier's uniform.

The Enslaved Journey to Britain

Crossing the Atlantic

The transatlantic slave trade involved three continents, Europe, Africa and the Americas; the Caribbean was included in the Americas. Traders would leave from the European ports such as Bristol, Liverpool and London when travelling to Africa for the exchange of goods, much of these exchanges included the bartering of slaves according to the Davenport papers.

Africans that were captured and forced into slavery crossed the Atlantic in ships where their journey was known as the 'Middle Passage'. Upon arrival in the Caribbean, those that survived the journey would be sold and put to work, which was more often than not, manual labour on plantations.

The ships would then return with goods such as sugar, rice, coffee and tobacco that were in high demand in Europe. Because George was still a baby, the accounts of his journey were not only undocumented, but the lack of witnesses to his journey leaves us with more questions than answers. However, to better understand the conditions in which this infant would have been transported, we have summarised accounts from a Zong journey which was a documented slave ship among many other slave ships.

The accounts paint a tear-jerking picture and it pains us as a society to think that an infant had suffered such a journey. The stark lack of regard for human life was brought into sharp focus with the legal case of the British slave ship, the Zong in 1783. The Zong left Africa with 442 slaves in September 1781. Due to navigation errors the ship missed its destination and spent more time at sea than expected which resulted in both food and water being in short supply.

With the fear of losing profits and having extra financial costs, 132 enslaved people were thrown into the sea by the crew so that an insurance claim could be made by the Liverpool ship-owners against the underwriters in Jamaica where the ship docked. Although these journeys were insured; much like commodities, losses at sea (by drowning) were covered, however, illness and starvation were not.

This meant that losses were more important than human health. A sad thought is that today's pet transport insurance is more humane than the 1800s slave transportation. If a slave jumped overboard the insurance company would pay out but if a slave died it would not! The legal case was made by the owners stating that to prevent the spread of disease they had to throw the sick enslaved Africans overboard, when in truth it was clear that it was just a ruse to ensure that the claim was successful.

Sadly, due to the lawful act that permitted sick animals on board a ship to be killed, of which was also accepted for the enslaved to be treated as the same that governed the transport of the enslaved on board; their claim was successful nonetheless. The murders of enslaved African people on the Zong sparked much discussion and action to end the British Slave Trade.

The treatment and suffering of captured Africans can be found in the surgeons' ship logs of Atlantic voyages. Although it is the perspective of the surgeon, it is a source of information to understand what happened on these voyages. The surgeon's role on board was to keep the enslaved alive to ensure there was no loss of profit before reaching the destination. Christopher Bowes was a surgeon on the Lord Stanley ship in 1788 and he kept journals that documented illnesses such as dysentery and smallpox.

The aim was to deliver healthy slaves for profit; however, they were only provided with the bare minimum daily rations of food and water which included yam, rice and beans. Many died of diseases on these ships or jumped overboard, drowning in the sea rather than facing a life of servitude.

It was documented that overcrowding, no sanitation and poor ventilation were the norm for the slave ships. They were well known for the sewer stench that emanated from them. Women and children were kept separately from the men who were shackled together in a coordinated manner.

However, the subtle freedom of women and children were not for their safety but rather for the convenience of the enslavers to abuse them at will.

It is recorded that more than twelve million enslaved Africans were taken across the 'Middle Passage' of the Atlantic between 1450 and 1850. There are very few personal accounts of the ordeal experienced by Africans on the slave ships that have been documented.

The Beautiful Spotted Boy

Documented experiences of enslaved people are very rare because it wasn't permitted. Despite the enslaved having their own languages, the practice of documenting their experiences was banned. This was crucial for the proslavery campaigns as the lack of documented accounts gave them the upper hand when called out on their actions.

One such preserved journey was that of Olaudah Equiano (c. 1745–1797), known for most of his life as Gustavus Vassa which was the name given to him by his first owner, Henry Pascal who was a Royal Navy officer of a British trading ship.

It is speculated that Equiano was kidnapped in what is now known as Nigeria, although in Equiano records it is confirmed that he was enslaved at the age of 11 and his first placement originating in the Caribbean. He was sold three times before he purchased his freedom in 1766. Equiano wrote his life story depicting his experiences detailing many of the horrors of slavery. Although he used the name imposed on him throughout his life, he published his autobiography under his birth name.

His life story became an anti-slavery testimonial while he campaigned for the abolishment of the slave trade. Unfortunately for George, being born on a plantation such a personal family name which Olaudah Equiano had received from his parents was not a luxury George had the privilege of having.

This is a classic example of the humiliation and the dehumanisation that the slave trade imposed on so many families. Equiano's first-hand graphic account of life onboard a slave ship demonstrates the inhuman treatment and the record of it forced the ignorant to take note.

"I was soon put down under the decks, and there I received such a salutation in my nostrils as I had never experienced in my life; so that, with the loathsomeness of the stench, and crying together, I became so sick and low that I was not able to eat, nor had I the least desire to taste anything.

I now wished for the last friend, death, to relieve me; but soon, to my grief, two of the white men offered me eatables; and on my refusing to eat, one of them held me fast by the hands and laid me across I think the windlass, and tied my feet, while the other flogged me severely."

The Interesting Narrative of the Life of Olaudah Equiano, aka Gustavus Vassa, the African, First published in 1789 in London

George's voyage might not have carried the same challenges as the slaves faced on the Zong or Equiano's voyage. It is understood from various sources that George was a 15-month-old baby when he was brought to England by Richard Gratton, who was a slave and plantation owner and overseer.

If this was the case, several accounts had led to believe George was transported on the 'Friendly Emma' vessel. The vessel was known to drop off and collect slaves and other cargo at St. Vincent and the Grenadines before its arrival in Bristol, England.

No detailed documentation has been uncovered regarding the ship logs or passengers during the believed time of George's arrival in 1809. However, it is documented that the Friendly Emma was shipwrecked in 1813 while travelling from St. Vincent and the Grenadines to Bristol. Coincidently the same year George died.

According to the account the wreck was found near the 'Scilly Isles' and the crew members were saved by Lady Sherbooke of Halifax.

The Enslaved Journey to Britain

Image: Author unknown. Courtesy of Bristol Record Office

Bristol Harbour circa 1850

The slave trade became a fundamental way of life for the economic success of Britain throughout the 1700s. Thousands of slave trade voyages were made to Africa from the late 1600s to the early 1800s.

Ports in London, Bristol and Liverpool were the most actively used for the transatlantic slave trade shipping companies' docking requirements.

The ports were the first locations in Europe for millions of African slaves who were trafficked. Many families found wealth by taking advantage of colonial slavery in the Caribbean and with the wealth bought land where they built large houses.

George was one of the unfortunate souls who had the misfortune of being born on a plantation owned by one of these families. It is still debatable whether George ultimately was sent to England alone or if his parents had accompanied him.

However, it is more than likely that his parents had not been with him because the plantation owners would have already had reassignments planned for them long before his birth. Still, it's daunting to think that as slave parents they would have no control over where their children would grow up or what life they would lead.

A large number of the wealthy families used the profits they made by exploiting the slave trade to invest in various industries and banking. Most of those investments played a role in the commercial, physical and political legacies of today.

Unlike their legacy, and their mark on the world today, it is still a struggle to find any records of George's family after he was transported to England.

Might this be because George was baptised as Richard and Catherine Gratton's own child? Or might it just be another way for the slave trade had stolen George's identity like done with so many others whereby their name was also taken to detach them from their identity.

In 2020, The National Trust published the 'Colonialism and Historic Slavery Report' on the houses built by plantation owners such as Sir William Young Bt 1st. This documented their enslaved household staff, yet, although many of the enslaved people's origins were not documented in the reports, like George, there are still many names and family lines that just disappeared from the records.

Britain and its Spotted Boy

George's arrival in Britain Bristol was not confirmed at the time of the project that SV2G delivered. However, it is believed to have been around either August or early September 1809 that Catherine and Richard Gratton arrived in England from St. Vincent with George.

Apart from the baptism certificate for George, there are no official records that the Gratton family had him in their care. There were also no official records of George being sold to Richardson. The exact details of how John Richardson, a theatre showman from Marlow in Buckinghamshire, took ownership of George, are still unknown.

There are journal accounts that claim George was bought by Richardson with an arrangement to be in his care for three years. The wording in the journal reads as follows:

"This remarkable child was born in the island of St.Vincent, in 1808; his parents were natives of Africa, and both black; the child's skin and hair were spotted or mottled all over dark-brown and white it was brought to Bristol when only fifteen months old, and an arrangement made with Richardson for its exhibition. The showman

took an affectionate interest in the child, and had it christened Geo. Alex. Gratton."

The Book of Days 1802-1871, Robert Chambers

The Book of Days article is a testament to the character of John Richardson in that, although it claims Richardson had affection for George, the journal account itself refers to George as less than human as he is referred to as 'it' or the 'spotted boy' rather than by his name.

This shows the bias and lack of transparency in the records of George's true story. Although it was widely reported in news articles that Richardson allegedly paid 1,000 guineas for George who was referred to as 'his spotted boy'. At the time that amount was viewed as a fortune.

Furthermore, research has enlightened us to the fact that George had not only been stripped of his identity, but also the mere privileged of being viewed as human was as well. The news articles from that time have portrayed George as nothing more than property.

We will never know if it was because of heartfelt emotions from Richardson towards George that caused him to pay so much for George as a slave. It was entirely unheard of for someone to pay so much for purchasing a slave let alone for hiring a slave.

Even though the debate is that he either overpaid or promised care for George. The fact remains that Richardson's choice to exploit George by displaying him for long hours, day and night proved that Richardson's cruelty saw no end; if it meant he could make more money.

It was also claimed that George was just placed in the care of Richardson for three years, without him being purchased, however the lack of accurate records makes it hard to find the real story.

If it is true that George was supposedly placed in Richardson's care, and that no cash was exchanged, it is even shocking to think that George's family entrusted their child to a man so cruel as to promise good care, yet lead George to his premature death.

Sadly, this still happens to children all around the world today, and the problem spans across all races and ages.

There is more than likely one household in your community that holds such an exploit today.

It might not be to the same extent, but child negligence and abuse comes in all forms. For George it was both being exposed to the cruelty of being judged on display and ripped from his family.

Human Commodity

George Alexander Gratton - "The Spotted Boy"

George Alexander Gratton was born with a skin condition known then as piebaldism; there was more superstition about the condition than facts and even though today it is still something that people sneer at. In the 1800s this condition was thought to be a curse and thus it created even more of a spectacle. The genetic condition piebaldism causes discolouration of skin pigmentation leading to extreme white patches all over a person's body and hair.

According to 'The Cabinet of Curiosities' (1851), George was born on 24 July 1808 in St. Vincent on a sugarcane plantation owned by William Alexander. The plantation was overseen by Richard Gratton. SV2G discovered that at the time of George's birth there were two plantation estates in one region owned by two different people with the same name - William Alexander.

One of the William Alexander plantation owners was a local resident of St. Vincent who travelled to England in 1813, coincidently the year George died, and he subsequently died there in 1814. The second plantation owner also named William Alexander was the son of Claud Alexander of Southbar who became paymaster-general for the East India Company in St Vincent. He later returned to Britain and bought Ballochmyle House and Estate (1795-1853).

Both men named William Alexander left legacies of owning enslaved people in St. Vincent and are also mentioned in the slavery compensation records at the University College London, Centre for the Study of the Legacies of British Slavery.

It is believed that George's mother could have been an enslaved African woman on the sugarcane plantation overseen by Gratton. Although we have the link to the name William Alexander as the plantation owner, it is still only the link to Gratton that is clear. Due to the lack of clarity of who George's parents were there is still research being done.

Like other enslaved Africans, George was likely to have been named after the sugar plantation's owner or overseer, a common practice at the time that identified enslaved people as the property of their owners. It was also reported in the Literary Journal in 1819 that George was shown in his 'native land' at the price of a dollar. The lack of clarity in the records leaves much room for speculation and is another testament to how little George meant to the communities that he was a part of.

Like a toy in the storefront that is only valued as long as the season permits, George's life records are both rare and vague. One line – his entire value summed up to one line in a journal and a single dollar. Whether this has any truth to it we do not know. However, the report claims that George would be more valuable as an exhibit abroad.

It is claimed, but no evidence found, that George's parents agreed that he should be sent to England although we know that during those times he would most likely have been taken regardless of parental consent.

It is noted, however, that Richard Gratton and his wife or partner Catherine, could have arrived in England from St. Vincent with George. There is a possibility that George would still have been in their care in London before being placed with John Richardson for three years.

Richard Gratton had commissioned Daniel Orme to paint a portrait of George in November 1809 that was published as 'George Alexander'. When George was baptised at Newington Church, Surrey on 22 July 1810, it was widely assumed that John Richardson had George baptised and this was used as evidence of his kind affection for George.

However, according to baptism records held at Southwark Library, Richard Gratton gave George his last name as George was listed as 'the illegitimate child of Richard and Catherine Gratton, a slave'. It is interesting to note firstly, the entry states Catherine Gratton as a slave and not Richard Gratton.

Secondly, Richard Gratton would have been in the country at the time George arrived and before baptising him as he had commissioned Daniel Orme to paint a life portrait of George which Gratton published on 11 November 1809 detailing his name as 'George Alexander'. Finally, many sources suggest both George's parents were enslaved; this may not have been the case, as is demonstrated in the baptism entry record.

Richardson's Spotted Boy Gimmick

When George arrived in England at Bristol port on the 'Friendly Emma' ship in 1809 aged just 15 months, he was at some point placed in the care of the famous showman John Richardson, originally from Marlow, Buckinghamshire.

Allegedly the Showman Richardson had paid 1,000 guineas for George which was viewed as a fortune at that time. George was not the first boy to be exploited by Richardson at the time, as he had displayed enslaved Africans at his shows before George was born. One of the other children that Richardson had exploited was John Bobey, born in Kingston, Jamaica.

Bobey was brought to England as a child by Liverpool merchant Mr Blundell. Bobey was subsequently baptised as 'John Richardson Primrose Bobey' and later bought and exhibited at fairs by a showman Mr Clarke.

Described as 'The Wonderful Spotted Indian', he was presented to the Royal Family at Windsor amongst others. Bobey was born in 1772 in Kingston, Jamaica with the skin disorder, stated as vitiligo.

It is referenced in the manuscript note presented to the Library of Philadelphia in the museum of Surgeon, T. Pole, Grace Church, in London that Bobey's parents were both enslaved black people stationed near Kingston, where he was discovered by a merchant named Mr Blundell.

Bobey was transported to Liverpool at the age of twelve and later he was bought as an exhibit called 'a scientific oddity'. Bobey was shown at fairs by showman Mr Clarke, including Richardson's theatre show at Bartholomew's fair in 1795. It is recorded that Bobey gained his freedom but continued to exhibit himself to earn a living.

According to the Royal College of Surgeons of England; Bobey, also known as 'The Spotted Indian' had married an English woman; apparently they had both continued working in shows together exhibiting in England and Scotland.

The engraving below, was thought to be made as part of William Granger's 'The New Wonderful Museum' in 1903, London. It also included various descriptions and portraits of a large number of 'extraordinary' people.

The Beautiful Spotted Boy

*An engraved portrait of John Bobey,
a black man with a skin pigmentation condition*

Bobey, John Primrose Richardson, 1803, showman
Courtesy of the Royal College of Surgeons

Life in Richardson's care for George

George lived with John Richardson in Horsemonger lane, London when he became part of Richardson's show. One showing of George was at Bartholomew Fair in Smithfield, London where George was displayed attracting monumental crowds. Richardson had a theatre booth that charged an admission fee to see George on display. During the intervals of plays and other entertainments, George would be advertised using headlines such as:

- 'A Negro Boy from the Caribbe Islands'
- 'The Wonderful Spotted Boy'
- 'The Beautiful Spotted Boy'
- 'An Extraordinary Spotted Boy'
- The 'Spotted Negro of Renown'
- 'A Live Curiosity Piece'

The National Archives describes George as 'a focus for the fascination in the 18th and 19th centuries with prodigies of nature, such as bearded women, living skeletons, seal boys, fairy children, and the like' at Bartholomew's Fair in Smithfield, London. According to advertisements about George, his hours of work were long, as he was available 'from 11am in the morning to dusk in the evening' appearing in areas such as Piccadilly and The Strand in London and Canterbury in Kent.

George was a frequent visitor to Marlow with John Richardson and according to sources he was displayed at the Marlow Fair. It is contentious as to whether slave auctions were held in Higginson Park before the Fair. It is very likely that George may have also been on private display to the Royal Family after such festivals.

A flyer advertising George on display at Richardson's home and available for other private viewings.

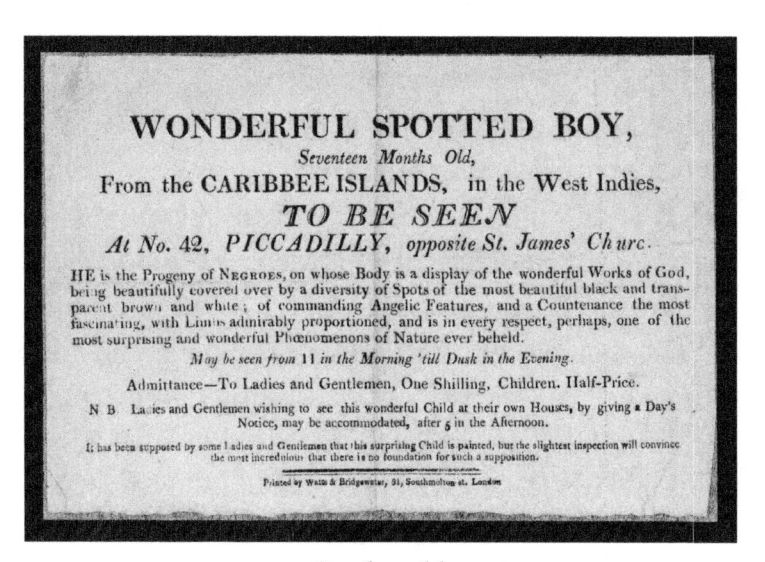

WONDERFUL SPOTTED BOY,
Seventeen Months Old,
From the CARIBBEE ISLANDS, in the West Indies,
TO BE SEEN
At No. 42, PICCADILLY, opposite St. James' Churc.

HE is the Progeny of NEGROES, on whose Body is a display of the wonderful Works of God, being beautifully covered over by a diversity of Spots of the most beautiful black and transparent brown and white; of commanding Angelic Features, and a Countenance the most fascinating, with Limbs admirably proportioned, and is in every respect, perhaps, one of the most surprising and wonderful Phœnomenons of Nature ever beheld.

May be seen from 11 in the Morning 'till Dusk in the Evening.

Admittance—To Ladies and Gentlemen, One Shilling. Children, Half-Price.

N B Ladies and Gentlemen wishing to see this wonderful Child at their own Houses, by giving a Day's Notice, may be accommodated, after 5 in the Afternoon.

It has been supposed by some Ladies and Gentlemen that this surprising Child is painted, but the slightest inspection will convince the most incredulous that there is no foundation for such a supposition.

Printed by Watts & Bridgewater, 91, Southmolton st. London

Produced by Watts & Bridgewater, London

George's popularity grew so much that he was frequently booked by the wealthy for private viewings in their homes. Consequently, he endured long days on display for twelve hours on most days which was likely to have affected his health. Unfortunately, George died on 3 February 1813 at the age of four years and nine months, never to see his family and homeland again.

His death was reported in the news that after a long illness he had died of 'a gathering of the jaw', which may have been a facial tumour. It has been suggested that in contrast to the hot climate he came from, being exhibited for long hours outdoors in cold weather could have contributed to his illness.

According to accounts, Richardson kept George's body unburied for three months for fear of it being stolen and being exhibited; this fear stemmed from the growing fascination with George's uniqueness. Richardson finally brought George's body for burial to his hometown Marlow in Buckinghamshire, where he was buried in a customised brick vault with a lavish funeral on 12 April 1813 in All Saints Church-yard. There was however no sign of such a brick vault during the condition assessment from GEM conservation commissioned by SV2G in 2018.

Piebaldism

George's piebaldism was not unusual, as there were other black children and adults that were brought to England due to their different physical appearances of features, to be exhibited in travelling 'freak shows'. Piebaldism is a genetic skin condition that causes white spots or patches to the skin, most commonly on the head, and face that can appear symmetrically to both sides of the body. In most cases, the condition is visible from birth, with many of those affected having a section of white hair at the front of their hairline.

Piebaldism can also easily be mistaken for other skin conditions such as Waardenburg syndrome, albinism, and vitiligo, all which have similar effects on the pigmentation. Waardenburg syndrome has additional symptoms and other genetic conditions along with the pigmentation of the skin. It is also worth noting that people with vitiligo are not always born with this condition, as it is acquired later in life. The term 'piebald' is still used today to describe animals with black and white spots or patches to their bodies. During the 18th century, the term was also used and what it viewed as an insulting way to describe what was considered a mismatch. The current language was no different then, than what it is now. It raises the question of why we still use these offensive terms to describe people's skin conditions in today's society.

The appearance of Piebaldism could be mistaken for Vitiligo, a similar skin condition that is still being researched today. An image of a portrait titled 'Our Little Variegated Damsel' was used in lectures to demonstrate skin conditions very similar to, if not the same, as George's. The painting was of Mary Sabina who was born on 12 October 1736 on Matuna plantation in Cartegena, Colombia. Her parents Martianiano and Patrona were enslaved on the plantation where she became famous locally.

An unknown local Columbian artist painted Sabina in 1740 and marked the portrait as a 'true picture of Marie'. Although Mary Sabina's image was circulated with great interest, it is believed that Sabina was the first known case of vitiligo, and according to the Hunterian Museum, Sabina was not known to have travelled to Europe. It is believed that the English factory owners on the plantation sent her unsigned portrait to London where it still hangs today in the Hunterian Museum of the Royal College of Surgeons.

A 'Live Curiosity Piece' to be seen

John Richardson – The Showman

John Richardson was brought up in a workhouse in Marlow, Buckinghamshire and became a farm labourer before he started his career as an actor when he joined Mrs. Penley's travelling theatre company in 1782.

Richardson eventually moved to London and became a broker, after which in 1798 he raised enough money to open his own travelling theatre company where he produced travelling theatrical shows.

He lived in Horsemonger Lane, Newington, Surrey, which is now called Harper Road in the borough of Southwark. The Road was notoriously known for a local prison for people that had housing debts and many other criminal charges.

When Richardson took ownership of George, they both lived on this road until his death. Richardson died in 1837 and requested in his will to be buried in the same vault with George. Richardson donated a painting of George that he had commissioned by the artist Coventry.

The beautiful painting is in immaculate condition at the All Saints Church in Marlow where it remains to this day. There are other accounts that claim it was Richardson's family that donated the painting when Richardson died.

In an article in 1901 in the South Bucks Herald, it was discovered that General Sir George Higginson wanted to sell the painting to raise funds for repairs to the church.

It was also reported that Richardson descendants objected and demanded that the painting be returned to them if the church no longer wished to display the portrait of George.

Marlow, Buckinghamshire

All Saints Church, Marlow, Buckinghamshire

SV2G, 2017

Marlow Town was a medieval town and was surrounded by land that was managed in the traditional strip system of open field farming that had existed for centuries. The Town today, is still laid out in its original design, with borage plots on either side of the High Street and a bridge across the Thames by the church.

The original All Saints Church where George was buried dates back to the 19th century that was built in replace of the previous Norman church which was originally situated closer to the river and was liable to flooding. The 18th-century mansion 'Remnantz' was located in West Street, and later became the home of the Wethered family, known for their local brewery company. It was known for one of the early locations of the Royal Military College before it moved to Sandhurst.

Marlow is also famously known for poet T. S. Eliot who also lived in West Street, during his time as a teacher at the High Wycombe Royal Grammar School. With its beautiful setting in the Chilterns, Marlow has also attracted many other artists and writers such as Mary Shelley where she completed 'Frankenstein'.

Marlow Fair dates back to the 17th century and in the past, it was held each year at the end of October along the streets of the town. It is believed that Richardson took George to the Marlow Fair on many occasions and displayed him to the public.

The SV2G team, are researching more about Richardson and his life in 1808, we hope to find more clarity on his own experience as a workhouse child labourer in Marlow.

Visit www.georgealexandergratton.com

Bartholomew Fair

Bartholomew Fair was where Richardson's first theatrical production was showcased in 1798. He used scenery from Drury Lane to turn the colourful and narrow booths into stunning stages for theatre performances.

Bartholomew's Fair was held in London each year over two weeks during the months of August and September. It was one of the largest events of its kind and became a fashionable setting for public entertainment in Britain.

Thousands of visitors attended each year to witness the many spectacles on show for their entertainment and enjoyment. The fair showcased plays, exhibited exotic animals and extraordinary people as well as selling a variety of food and alcohol.

The increased connections with Britain and the continent created the opportunity for Black people to be transported from Africa and the Caribbean to be displayed in these shows. Known by many as 'travelling freak shows', people from all races and nationalities would be selected to be exhibited as freaks of nature.

This was due to their physical abnormalities as a fascination grew in the 18th and 19th centuries for viewing 'curiosities' such as bearded women, a giant Irishman, seal boys and Saartjie Baartman a Khoikhoi woman who was exhibited alongside George who was headlined as 'a spotted Negro Boy from the Caribbee'. Saartjie Baartman, also known as Sarah Baartman, was a Khoikhoi woman born in 1789 in a village in the Cape Colony, South Africa. At the age of 20 years old, she was brought to London by William Dunlop, a British ship doctor.

As in the case of George Gratton and Saartjie Baartman, Dunlop viewed Baartman as a lucrative venture to make money according to evidence presented by Zachary Macaulay, a London Merchant. Dunlop displayed Baartman as a 'freak of nature'.

Crude images of her were depicted by cartoonist George Cruikshank who would exaggerate her features. When Baartman died in 1816, her body parts were preserved in French museums until her remains were returned to her homeland, after an agreement made between President Nelson Mandela of South Africa and President François Mitterrand of France in 1994.

*Richardson's travelling booth at
Camberwell Fair, London*

Source unknown

Although, Richardson's shows were all over London such as Camberwell, Southwark, and Greenwich he became so popular and toured throughout England. Richardson's travelling theatre shows became so famous whereby Gilbert and Sullivan's Colonels sang of them in 'Patience'. Charles Dickens (182-1870) also wrote about Richardson's shows in 'Sketches by Boz'. Dickens described Richardson's booth;

A 'Live Curiosity Piece' to be seen

"This immense booth, with the large stage in front, so brightly illuminated with variegated lamps, and pots of burning fat, is 'Richardson's', where you have a melodrama (with three murders and a ghost), a pantomime, a comic song, an overture, and some incidental music, all done in five-and-twenty minutes."

Charles Dickens

'Sketches by Boz', is a collection of short articles and stories about London, they were published in sections that first appeared around 1833, and then in 1836 as a full collection of Dickens' works.

The noise, atmosphere and scenes at the Bartholomew Fair with other acts including animals, all in close proximity to each other, had to have been a frightening experience for George. We will never know his feelings and experiences about having to perform in this disgraceful manner.

Many shows and displays such as Richardson's shows were considered an acceptable pastime that became inappropriate, during the 18th and 19th centuries. These big fairs became unpopular due to the offensive debauchery that was constantly witnessed at the fairs. London authorities were concerned about these scandalous vulgar theatre shows. These events at Bartholomew Fair were believed to be preventing the working class from their employment due to the large quantity of alcohol that was being consumed. Eventually, after a number of public disturbances, they were banned from the site in 1855.

The background to 'The Microcosm of London' collection of prints can be found in three published volumes from 1808 to 1910. The publisher Rudolph Ackermann collaborated with cartoonist and illustrator Thomas Rowlandson and architectural draughtsman Auguste Charles Pugin to produce colourful prints.

As a successful commercial publishing company, The Microcosm of London supplied high-coloured prints of everyday themes. Today, these prints are recognised as interesting historical accounts of life in Georgian society in London.

Richardson Theatre production stage at Bartholomew Fair can be seen in the image. It was first shown and issued separately then was collated into separate volumes with other prints that have proven to be a very profitable enterprise for the publisher.

A 'Live Curiosity Piece' to be seen

Illustration of John Richardson's Booth at Bartholomew Fair in Smithfield, outside St Bartholomew's Hospital, London.

The Microcosm of London, a collection of prints 1808 to 1910 Ackerman's Microcosm of London 1808

Portrait Commissions of George Alexander Gratton

There are two known commissioned paintings of George Alexander Gratton that have been recorded and are available to view today. Richard Gratton commissioned the first portrait of George by Daniel Orme. Orme painted George 'from life' and the painting was published on 11 November 1809. This means Orme must have met George shortly after his arrival in England.

The painting depicts little George sitting on a turtle near a Dalmatian dog whereby the viewer can compare the two by juxtaposing George's skin disorder with that of a Dalmatian dog that has a similar spotted skin.

The painting was later engraved under Orme's direction by his then pupil, P R Cooper. The writing beneath the painting confirms that it was published by 'Richard Gratton Esquire, London'. The painting was sold by Orme from his address at 368, Oxford Street, London. Copies of the engraving were later sold as souvenirs to those who visited the exhibitions to stare at poor George.

A 'Live Curiosity Piece' to be seen

"George Alexander, a black boy with white markings" by P.R. Cooper, sold by and after Daniel Orme coloured etching and aquatint, published 11 November 1809."

*By courtesy of the:
The WellcomeLibrary, London*

Daniel Orme was a painter and engraver born in Manchester who studied at the Royal College of Art. His studio at 308 Oxford Street in London was the location where George must have been when he was painted. His work usually depicted popular military persons such as Lord Nelson including Olaudah Equiano's portrait that was used in his autobiography.

The National Portrait Gallery stated:

"This is a historic work of art which reflects the attitudes and viewpoints of the time in which it was made. Whilst these may differ from today's attitudes, this image is an important historical document. This image is currently being researched, further information about this image will be updated below."

The second painting was commissioned by John Richardson and was painted by Coventry in 1811. After Richardson died, the painting was given to the County of Buckinghamshire.

The oil painting remained in All Saints Church in Marlow and continues to draw attraction today. The image of George is considered to be deceiving, as he is portrayed much older than what he would have been.

A 'Live Curiosity Piece' to be seen

The portrait of George Alexander, painted from life in 1811, commissioned by John Richardson and given to the County of Buckinghamshire after he died.

By courtesy of the All Saints Church, Marlow, Buckinghamshire

The Spotted Negro Boy

Cabinet of Curiosities c 1851

The above sketch depicts George Alexander Gratton in 1851, if this was a true genuine likeness of George, it would mean he would be in his 50's. If this was the case, we would question if George died at the age of 4 years old.

Death and Burial

The Royal College of Surgeons

According to reports in the press, George was attended by four doctors from the Royal College of Surgeons.

These were;
- Dr Dundas of Richmond,
- Dr Astley Cooper of the City,
- Mr Phillips of Southward,
- Mr Scott of Bromley, Kent.

When George died on 3 February 1813, one press article concluded with;

"after a lingering suffering for a considerable time, departed this life, in consequence of a gathering in the jaw"

It is also suggested from the researched information available at the time and various sources claimed that a sum of money was exchanged by Richardson for George to be in his care for three years. The amount reported varies with no substantiated evidence to support this.

What is consistent are the claims of George being in Richardson's care for three years and that coincidentally he died just after his final appearance as advertised widely in national newspapers.

George Alexander Gratton Death Announcement

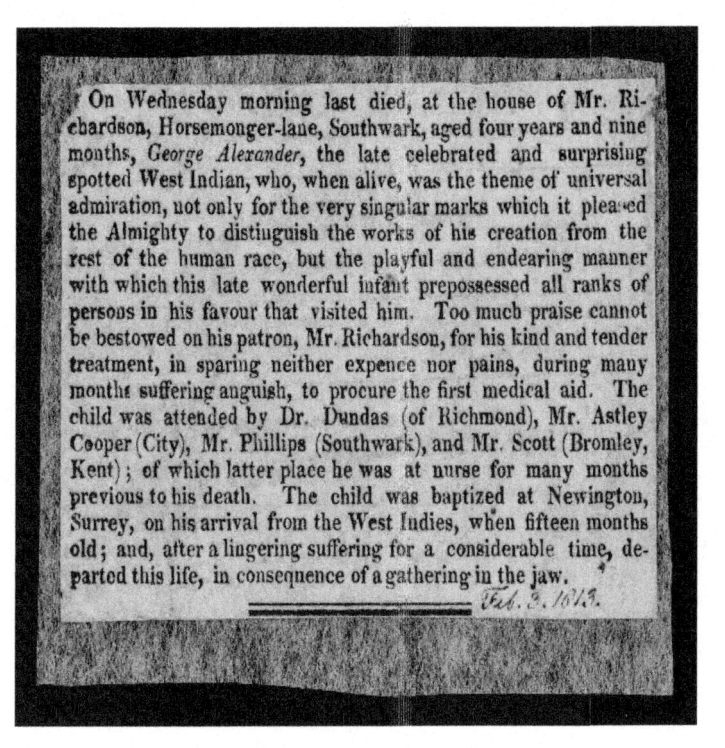

> On Wednesday morning last died, at the house of Mr. Richardson, Horsemonger-lane, Southwark, aged four years and nine months, George Alexander, the late celebrated and surprising spotted West Indian, who, when alive, was the theme of universal admiration, not only for the very singular marks which it pleased the Almighty to distinguish the works of his creation from the rest of the human race, but the playful and endearing manner with which this late wonderful infant prepossessed all ranks of persons in his favour that visited him. Too much praise cannot be bestowed on his patron, Mr. Richardson, for his kind and tender treatment, in sparing neither expence nor pains, during many months suffering anguish, to procure the first medical aid. The child was attended by Dr. Dundas (of Richmond), Mr. Astley Cooper (City), Mr. Phillips (Southwark), and Mr. Scott (Bromley, Kent); of which latter place he was at nurse for many months previous to his death. The child was baptized at Newington, Surrey, on his arrival from the West Indies, when fifteen months old; and, after a lingering suffering for a considerable time, departed this life, in consequence of a gathering in the jaw.
> *Feb. 3. 1813.*

Bells Weekly Messenger 7th February 1813

Death and Burial

According to several accounts, Richardson kept George's body unburied for three months for fear of it being stolen. George was eventually buried in a customised brick vault with a lavish funeral on 12th April 1813 in the home town of Richardson at All Saints Church, Marlow, Buckinghamshire. There was however no sign of such a brick vault during the recent conservation assessment commissioned by SV2G.

A Headstone with an engraved epitaph and a footstone with the letters 'G.A.G.' marks George's grave. In Richardson's will, he requested for his body to be buried in the same vault as George in 1837. It is believed that Richardson's last wishes would have been carried out by his executor Mr Edward Cross.

However, there are no records of Richardson being buried in the same plot as George or anywhere in the church-yard. It is believed that Richardson's remains are most likely in a vault that was built around the new church.

There are limited playbills and flyers available today of shows that George appeared in. However, one significant flyer that is held in the Wellcome

Library details George having his final season in the country.

The image was replicated as an emblem on George's headstone and believed to be the same image Richardson used to produce flyers for George's funeral that he had distributed to the public. It has been reported that Edward Battening, Marlow ironmongers kept George's print that was given out to mourners attending George's funeral.

The print has been held in the Battening family and was passed down from generation to generation along with other historic memorabilia and journals over a period of 150 years, added to by four generations.

The church vestry is reported to have been where Richardson kept Georges' body for three months. It is thought that Richardson built a vault for George with his intention to be buried with him as indicated in his will.

Image of a Playbill – Richardson's New Theatre

By courtesy of the Wellcome Library

Epitaphs and Inscriptions

The gravestone and tribute to George's life today in Marlow, marks the grave of one of the earliest recorded bonds between an enslaved child from St. Vincent and Marlow. There are many epitaphs and inscriptions on headstones that visually document early Black presence in England today.

The following epitaph was commissioned by John Richardson for George's gravestone.

TO THE MEMORY OF
GEORGE ALEXANDER GRATTON,
THE SPOTTED NEGRO BOY,

From the Caribbe Islands, in the West Indies
A Native of the Carribee Islands, in the West Indies.
Who departed this life February 3d, 1813,
Aged four years and three quarters. This Tomb, erected
by his only Friend and Guardian,
Mr. John Richardson, of London.

Should this plain simple tomb attract thine eyes,
Stranger, as thoughtfully thou passest by,
Know that there lies beneath this humble stone,
A child of colour, haply not thine own.

His parents born of Afric's sun-burnt race,
Tho' black and white were blended in his face,
To Britain brought, which made his parents free,
And shew'd the world great Natur's prodigy.

Depriv'd of kindred that to him were dear,
He found a friendly Guardian's fost'ring care,
But, scarce had bloom'd, the fragrant flower fades,
And the lov'd infant finds an early grave,
To bury him his lov'd companions came,
And drop't choice flowers, and lis'd his early fame;
And some that lov'd him most, as if unblest,
Bedwe'd with tears the whice wreath on his breast.
But he is gone, and dwells in the abode,
Where some of every clime must joy in God!

In comparison with George's inscription, Anna Maria Vassa, the daughter of Olaudah Equiano aka Gustavas Vassa's headstone is very similar.

However, Anna Maria died several months before her father on 21 July 1797, which is nearly 17 years before George yet the verses for her epilogue are very much alike. It is peculiar that both Anna and George died aged four years old. Anna is buried at St Andrews church in Chesterton, Cambridgeshire, a commemorative plaque is located on the wall outside the church.

The Beautiful Spotted Boy

The plaque of Anna Maria Vassa, contains the following verse;

"Should simple village rhymes attract thine eye,
Stranger, as thoughtfully thou passest by,
Know that there lies beside this humble stone,
A child of colour, haply not thine own.

Her father born of Afric's sun-burnt race,
Torn from his native fields, ah! foul disgrace;
Through various toils at length to Britain came,
Espous'd, so heaven ordain'd, an English dame,
And follow'd Christ their hope two infants dear,
But one, a Hapless Orphan, slumbers here.

To bury her, the village children came,
And dropp'd choice flowers, and lisp'd her early fame;
And some that lov'd her most, as if unblest.
Bedew'd with tears the white wreath on their breast.
But she is gone and dwell's in that abode,
Where some of every clime shall joy in God."

It is believed that the poet Martha Peckard wrote both epitaphs for Anna Maria and George, as Martha's husband Peter Peckard was a friend of Equiano and the Dean of Peterborough.

Conservation, Memorial and Plaque

The SV2G project included the cleaning and stabilisation of the headstone, footstone, and ledger, and incorporated additional new Portland stone kerb surrounds, and inscription panel.

As outlined in the commissioned condition report by GEM Conservation, the condition of the two limestone headstones, and one footstone made of Yorkstone, in order to assess causes of their deterioration.

To this end, a range of rapid assessment methods were used, including pH, conductivity, capacitance, liquid moisture, porosity, nitrate and chloride identification of the stones surfaces, substrates and soil conditions. It was clear that the three stones themselves are at various stages of deterioration from areas of advanced deterioration to minimal weathering.

George's headstone was particularly affected through intrinsic issues inherent in the structure and materials, combined with extrinsic influences, natural agents, and human activity.

GEM Conservation also reported on the main structural problem of the effect of historic two fractures across the face of the headstone, at ground level and just above the midpoint.

The ground level fracture has been repaired some years ago using traditional dog-cramp ties, with molten lead poured onto the cramp and its mortice recess for protection on both sides. The midpoint fissure was still open allowing weathering elements to ingress, but is effectively held in place by the effectiveness of the earlier dog cramp system.

The second type of defect related to both the shape and structure of the stone, and also the impact of weathering upon the relief carving morphology, influencing the repeated water flow and channelling of moisture down the stone to meet with ascending moisture from the ground.

The stone has been carved with the grain of the stone vertically face-bedded, which increases the absorption of environmental agents significantly.

John Richardson's headstone adjacent to George's headstone was made on its natural horizontal bedding plane.

George's headstone was believed to be made from a fine-grained Portland Basebed, whereas Richardson's is a coarser grain and more weather resistant Portland Whitbed.

No brick vault was located during the assessment of George Alexander Graton's grave.

The above information was taken from the SV2G Commissioned report on the condition of George's grave by Matthew Beasley, GEM Conservation at the start of the project.

"We came to the memorial stone project of George Alexander Gratton, from the ethical viewpoint that treatment would be contingent on respecting and understanding the social context of George and his unique culture. This was correlated to an understanding of the inherent decay mechanisms specific to the micro-climate of the headstone and the local environment.

A condition assessment was carried out, taking into account the dependence of the stone's condition on its history (hysteresis), and we were able to reveal specific areas of original black polychrome, indicating a carefully orchestrated composition.

Laser-scanning technology of surfaces disclosed information on the carved high relief detailing that was not possible to visualise under normal lighting conditions. Once this information was correlated to printed documentary sources, one could hypothesise quite strongly, upon the subject matter and composition of the missing section, (an Idealisation of George's homeland, drawn from paintings and documentary sources).

Understanding of the 'memory effect' of hysteresis, and the reduction of surface areas by utilising nano-lime technology, formed a major part of our Preventive Maintenance and Minimal Interventionist strategy for conservation. By this process, we were able to close the 'hysteresis loop'.

Symbolically, this may be also viewed as drawing the circle between the recent treatment of the biological and mineralogical/petrographic transformation of the stone, and the origin and source of George's biographical and social context, and extraordinary cultural Heritage, for the generations to come."

Matthew Beasley, GEM Conservation

John Richardson's Death and Will

On his deathbed in 1837, Richardson requested to be buried in the same vault as Gratton and this was detailed in his will. Some accounts suggest this was a reflection of the affection he felt for George and the 'parental kindness' he demonstrated.

This notion is however in sharp contrast to the cruel way in which the young child was exploited in his care. During the latter part of SV2G's project, before GEM conservation was able to lay the commemoration project plaque, confirmation was required that no other grave was located for the proposed site of the plaque. From viewing the plans for the layout of graves within the church-yard, the staff were able to confirm that there was no grave in situ of the proposed location for the project plaque.

It was also discovered that there was no evidence to be found that John Richardson was in the same grave as George.

Although Richardson's headstone can be found at the back of George's headstone there was no evidence to suggest where exactly Richardson's coffin is located within the church-yard.

Removal of the grave

As advised by one of Marlow Society's historians, he said:

"The point about the lack of the vault which John Richardson had built probably means that the grave has been moved, having originally been sited on the area cleared for the new church. When I was young all the walls round the back and side of the churchyard were lined with the stones removed from these graves, but the Rev. Vaughan Wilkes had most of them removed."

One answer that can be considered was during the flooding and rebuilding of the church, the grave had been moved from its original location.

This would also corroborate with the historical sources that described the grave located by the riverbank. The unanswered question would be where the remains of John Richardson now lay?

According to Richardson's will, a led coffin was requested and for his body to be buried in the same vault as George Alexander Gratton.

However, as indicated in SV2G's commissioned condition assessment from GEM conservation in 2018, no vault was found in the grave where George Alexander Gratton's headstone lies today.

In conclusion, it is believed that the new church was built around the original grave that houses the vault as described in various sources. Whether John Richardson is in the vault hence no record of his grave location in the church records, we do not know.

The preserved Grave of George Alexander Gratton

SV2G, 2019

"For he hath not despised nor abhorred the affliction of the afflicted; neither hath he hid his face from him; but when he cried unto him, he heard." Psalm 22.24

Timeline

Life and Legacy of George Alexander Gratton

- **July 1808**
  George Alexander Gratton is born on a sugarcane plantation on the island of St. Vincent and the Grenadines.

- **August / September 1809**
  George Alexander Gratton arrived in Bristol. It was reported that he was purchased for 1000 guineas by the travelling showman John Richardson, who exhibited him as an entertainment.

- **November 1809**
  Richard Gratton commissions a portrait of George. Painted from life by Daniel Orme and engraved under his direction by his late pupil P R Cooper, London.

- **July 1810**
  George is baptised at Newington Church, Surrey as George Alexander Gratton.

Timeline

- **November 1811**
  John Richardson commissions the portrait of George to be painted by Coventry.

- **February 1813**
  George Alexander Gratton dies of 'gathering of the jaw' in Newington Surrey, aged 4 years and 9 months.

- **April 1813**
  George is buried in All Saints Church, Marlow, Buckinghamshire

- **2007**
  George's skin pigmentation was featured in The Royal College of Surgeons, A Visable Difference: skin, race and identity Exhibition.

- **2018-2020**
  SV2G's Heritage Fund project and Exhibition on George Alexander Gratton.

  SV2G commissioned the preservation work on the grave of George Alexander Gratton, which was completed by GEM conservation.

Bibliography

Adams, E. (2002). People on The Move - The effects of Some Important Historical Events on the People of St. Vincent and the Grenadines. R & M Adams Book Centre.

Adams E. (2004). National Treasures. R & M Adams Book Centre.

Adams, E. (2010). The Carib Country Sugar Estates and Georgetown 1797-2010. R & M Adams Book Centre.

Adams, E. (2011). The African Presence and Influence on the Cultural Traditions of St. Vincent & the Grenadines. R & M Adams Book Centre.

Adams, E. (2014). The Making of the Dorsetshire Hill Community. R & M Adams Book Centre.

Chambers, R. (1869). The Book of Days: a miscellany of popular antiquities in connection with the calendar, including anecdote, biography and history, curiosities of literature, and oddities of human life and character. W & R Chambers.

Cugoano, O. (ed. Carretta, V.). (1999). Thoughts and Sentiments on the Evil of Slavery. Pengiun Books Inc.

Bibliography

Dabydeen, D. (1985). Hogarth's Blacks: Images of Blacks in Eighteenth Century English Art. Dangaroo Press.

Dickens, C. (1836). Sketches by Boz: Illustrative of Every-day Life and Every-day People. John Macrone.

Edwards, B. (1801). The History, Civil and Commercial, of the British Colonies in the West Indies 3rd edition. John Stockdale.

Edwards, P. and Dabydeen, D. (1991). Black Writers in Britain 1760-1890: An Anthology. Edinburgh University Press.

Edwards, P. and Walvin, J. (1983). Black Personalities in the Era of the Slave Trade. Palgrave Macmillan.

Edwards, P. and Rewt, P. (1994). The Letters of Ignatius Sancho. Indiana University Press.

Equiano, O. (2000). The Interesting Narrative of the Life of Olaudah Equiano, Or Gustavus Vassa, The African, 1789. Dover Publications.

Fraser, A. (2019). From Villain to National Hero; Chatoyer and the early struggle for the Independence of St. Vincent (Yurumein). Hobo Jungle Press.

Fryer, P. (1988). Black People in the British Empire. Pluto Press.

George Alexander Gratton Website. www.georgealexandergratton.com

Hulme, P, (1992). Colonial Encounters: Europe and the Native Caribbean. Routledge.

Hulme P. and Whitehead N. (1992). Wild Majesty: Encounters with the Caribs from Columbus to the Present Day. Oxford University Press.

Kirby L. E. and C.I. Marti. (1986). The Rise and Fall of the Black Caribs (Garifuna). Cybercom. (originally St. Vincent, 1985).

Le Breton, A. (1998). Historic Account of Saint Vincent, the Indian Youroumayn, the Island of the Karaybes, Edited by the Mayreau Environmental Development Organisation. Model Printery Ltd.

Odumosu, T. (2014). "Burthened Bodies": the Image and Cultural Work of "White Negroes" in the Eighteenth Century Atlantic World". American Studies in Scandinavia, 46.1: 31-53.

Odumosu, T (2011). "Exhibiting Difference": A Curatorial Journey with George Alexander Gratton the "Spotted Negro Boy" in Representing Enslavement and Abolition in Museums. Eds Smith, Laurajane, Geoff Cubitt et al. Routledge.

Bibliography

Reyahn King et al. (1997). Ignatius Sancho, an African Man of Letters. National Portrait Gallery.

Robinson, John, Side Show World Website, www.sidewhowworld.com

Shephard, C. (1997). An Historical Account of the Island of Saint Vincent 1831.Frank Cass & Co Ltd.

Sherson, E. (1925). "Richardson's Show and Other Theatrical Booths". London's Lost Theatres of the Nineteenth Century. John Lane The Bodley Head.

Shyllon, F. O. (1977). Black People in Britain 1555-1833. Oxford University Press.

Stanton, S, Banham, Martin, eds.
(1996). "Richardson's Show". The Cambridge Paperback Guide to Theatre. Cambridge University Press

SV2G Website. www.sv2g.org.uk

Taylor, C. (2012). The Black Carib Wars, Freedom, Survival and the Making of the Garifuna. Signal Books Ltd.

Unknown/Anonymous, (1840). The Cabinet of Curiosities, Or Wonders of the World Displayed: Forming a Repository of Whatever is Remarkable in the Regions of Nature and Art, Extraordinary

Eveny, and Eccentric Biography. With Forty-three Illustrations, Piercy and Reed.

Walvin, J. (1998). An African's Life: The Life and Times of Olaudah Equiano 1745-1797. Continuum.

Wood, M. (2000). Blind Memory: Visual Representations of Slavery in England and America 1780-1865. Manchester.

Young, Sir William, 1st Bart. (1764). Considerations which may tend to promote our new West India Colonies. James Robson.

Young, Sir William, 1st Bart. (2011). The West India Common Place Book: Compiled from Parliamentary and official Documents; Shewing the Interest of Great Britain in its Sugar Colonies 1807. Nabu Press.

Young, Sir William, 2nd. Bart. (1795). An Account of the Black Charaibs in the Island of St. Vincent's, J. Sewell; Cornhill; and Knight; and Triphook.

Printed in Great Britain
by Amazon